Thank God
and Take Courage

Thank God and Take Courage

Here I Am—Send Me

David C. Derby

LUCAS PARK BOOKS

ST. LOUIS, MISSOURI

Library of Congress Control Number:
ISBN: 978-1-60350-028-9

Published by Lucas Park Books
www.lucasparkbooks.com

Printed in the United States of America

Contents

Look!—No Training Wheels!

By Way Of Introduction

"You should write a book!" Or so I have been told by friends, acquaintances and Church members for many years. Looking back over fifty years of ministry the realization dawns that I do have many things to share. Although written from a personal perspective, the following pages are not as much about me as they are about Christian Ministry, the Church in the twentieth and twenty first centuries and the fascinating people—good, bad and in-between, who constitute the world and are a part of this thing we call life.

It is my hope that pastors and lay people alike will be amused but more importantly, enlightened, enriched and encouraged by the thoughts, insights and adventures accumulated over these many years and which continue to increase as each day unfolds. Life is a gift which is best enjoyed and appreciated as it is shared in the telling, but most of all in the living. The gift is first of all from God, but many others are an essential part of it The adults who nurtured us in childhood, people, wise and caring that we meet along the way and especially family and loved ones who know us best and love us anyway.

Ministry for me has been a partnership with Phyllis with whom I have shared over fifty years of marriage, ministry, blessing and joy. Her Love, help, patience and encouragement have made it not only worthwhile but possible. Besides bearing the joys and burdens every step of the way she is the one who keeps me down to earth, mindful of what is important and focused on the practical implications of Christ's message. For this I am grateful beyond words.

What Is This Really About?

"Not every one who says to me, 'Lord, Lord,' will enter the Kingdom of heaven, but only one who does the will of my Father who is in heaven." (MATTHEW 7:21)

I was always one for cutting through the nonsense and getting to the point. I am sure this is why I had little patience in seminary for the courses in Theology, Philosophy and Christian Doctrine. With all due respect to the likes of Tillich, Barth, Brunner, Neibuhr et.al I don't think Jesus intended to form a doctrine, a formula for "salvation" or a labyrinth of belief systems unapproachable and foreign to the people he so loved and tried to reach. Over the centuries the Church or some within the Church have formed structures, doctrines and systems that shut out more people than they invite in. There is too much concern for what is said and written about Jesus and too much neglect in understanding who Jesus was, what he said and what he did. If his death on the cross is to be truly honored, respected, appreciated and meaningful then remember, he died because he loved us to be sure but he loved us enough to stand up for what he said and how he lived. We best honor him and fulfill our own purposes when we set about to do what he said and did and not in becoming so concerned about the belief systems, the formulas for "salvation" and deciding among ourselves who gets to heaven and who doesn't because they don't happen to be just like us. The works of theologians and scholars may be useful in making us think or deepening our intellectual understanding but they are of little use to the advancement of the mission, message and hope set forth by Jesus Christ. The real point is, who exactly was Jesus, what did he tell us and what did he demonstrate to us by his life, death and resurrection. It is not about systems, plans of salvation and the papers issued by some theological think tank. Do I accept Jesus as Lord, Savior and Son of God?—Yes! Do I accept all the systems, claims and narrow interpretations of Jesus?—No! Like Albert Schweitzer, I believe that we should concern ourselves with the Quest for the historical Jesus and leave the speculation alone.

In 1986, two sisters in Mississippi were sentenced to unduly harsh life sentences for a small part in a robbery. In 2010 one of the sisters needed a kidney transplant and the other offered her kidney. The Governor of that state commuted the sentences on condition that the transplant take place. This was justice delayed but at least it made the best of a bad situation and addressed the human needs of the two sisters and brought justice to them at last. Immediately a group of ethical "experts" and professors were all over this questioning the motives and ethical implications of this. Why? What do these guys know of the real world and human need, suffering and injustice on the streets and beyond the classroom? We don't live in a perfect world but we can work for what is right under the circumstances we have. In short—stop talking and just do it.

The people that we are called on to serve in Christ's name and spirit do not live in ivory towers. They live in a real world that sometimes gets rough and is never under any conditions, perfect. It is that world where Jesus was criticized for going to dinner with folks from the "wrong side of the tracks" and for doing good things on the Sabbath. The criticism came from the people who never did much to help anybody. There is a common saying that I think is misguided and wrong.—"I would rather see a sermon than hear one." To me that is smug and narrow. What it is really saying is, "I'll be your judge. You do and I'll watch." It usually comes from people who don't bother to go to Church or who do not listen if they are there. Our calling is to do and not to judge.

Ministry is about taking the teaching, the love, the insights and the compassion of Jesus into the world we live in today. It means being a spokesperson for God through word and action. It can also mean being misunderstood. Surely there are risks. No one took more risks than Christ himself, still we are called to follow and to lead.

What is this really all about? It is about discovering what Jesus said and learning from what Jesus did and putting it to work in our lives and experience. As Jesus said to the rich young man who inquired about eternal life,

"Do this and you will live."

1

Defining The Church

"Now you are the body of Christ and individually, members of it." (I CORINTHIANS 12:27)

What is the Church? There is a challenge that is more difficult than it sounds. First of all to say "What is the Church?" is to ask the wrong question. The right question is, "Who is the Church?" While we may refer to the Church as God's Church or the Church of Jesus Christ, we are actually speaking of a body composed of human beings and all of the attendant flaws and imperfections that go with that circumstance. Persons outside the Church often look upon us as those who should be perfect. The fact is, the Church is not perfect; never was and never will be. Like all of God's creation, we are a work in progress.

We hear such terms as people of God or community of faith. Exactly who are the people of God? Who is the community of faith? We might define them as those who from the earliest days of Christian knowledge have formed groups or banded together to share faith and mission. This is no ordinary organization or club or family. In identifying ourselves as people of faith, followers of Christ, servants of God we establish a divine—human connection. There is something different about meeting for worship that sets it apart from meeting to discuss a book or settle a political issue or for a community service club. Worship places our focus on the divine and unites us in a spirit of faith. Worship is shared faith.

There are many more aspects of Church life than Sunday Worship. There is growth through learning, there is service to the community, there is compassion for the hurting world that leads to giving our resources and becoming informed and involved in the struggle for justice and peace. All of this comes from another shared resource, The Bible. The Bible eloquently describes our identity, nature and mission in these words from the First Letter of Peter:

> "But you are a chosen race, a royal priesthood, a holy nation, God's own people, in order that you might proclaim the mighty acts of him who called you out of darkness into his marvelous light. Once you were not a people, but now you are God's people; once you had not received mercy, but now you have received mercy." (I PETER 2:9–10)

That is a high sounding claim but hear it all. We are called all of this because we have a purpose and that purpose is to share with the world what we have experienced ourselves; the marvelous light and the mercy of God.

As much as we may admire the Church and desire to support it's sacred mission and message, we must face the fact that any institution made up of human beings will be imperfect. The Church is no exception. Over the course of my ministry I have held several denominational offices and positions of leadership in which we had to deal with issues of clergy misconduct, congregational schisms and bitter misunderstandings. In more recent years, I have been called upon to teach sessions for clergy in boundary awareness. This includes appropriate behavior in the work place, sexual harassment, financial integrity and the proper use of social media. Two generations ago, it would seem incredulous that such classes would be required or considered necessary.

For many perhaps they aren't but we have come a long way from the days when such things were swept under the carpet and denied. I honestly believe that some form of boundary awareness should be taught to congregations also. Many who piously claim to be devout Christians do not live or act out the love of Christ in their local Church. My denominational positions have also made it necessary to deal with congregational splits and battles. None of this is pleasant. All of it is real. Fortunately these issues are the exception and not the norm . They are certainly nothing new and unheard of. Read the New Testament and you will see. But in spite of its imperfections, misunderstandings and opposition, the Church survives because there is a hunger on our part for God and the love of God who continues to reach out to us imperfect human beings.

We are God's people but we are still human with our arguments in Church council meetings, our sometimes misplaced priorities, our failure to always love kindness or do justice and our mistakes along the way. Yet somehow with God's help the Church rises above all of this and becomes for us a spiritual family where we find nurture and faith.

Shortly after assuming the pastorate of one Church someone informed me that there was a person present in worship every Sunday who had declined membership saying, "I am not sure what I believe but if those Christians are right, I want to be there." My informant did not identify who this was but I was not long in figuring it out. Some time later, I approached her about becoming a member of the Church. The response was a laugh and a horrified look. Perhaps it is easy to admire faith but difficult to commit to the challenges and demands. I had occasion to read through some old meeting minutes of a congregation from the 1920's. It seems that during one meeting three men were asked to become deacons. The minutes reveal that two of these declined but the third said he would serve when he was present, if needed and if it was convenient. Wouldn't Jesus be proud! Yet in spite of our human weaknesses the Church goes on empowered by the Spirit of God who continues to call us out of darkness into the marvelous light.

Whether most of the world is aware of the need or even cares, whether or not there is a Church—God still calls people to come and experience the joy of believing and the challenge of sharing faith in worship and on the street.

There are many facets of Church life that make up the whole of who we are and what we represent. They are sometimes amusing, sometimes tragic and sometimes deeply touching. Faith is involved with all that we do in Church and in life. The Church touches our lives at birth, marriage, death, and at many other stops along the way. Of all institutions on earth it is most to be taken seriously. To those who claim that they do not associate with the Church because there are so many hypocrites there—I would say, true but they are God's hypocrites. What is more I truly believe that the worst hypocrites are the ones who say that.

In the Church we are blessed with opportunity to share deeply in the divine-human encounter and to enter into a realm of compassion and service unknown to most. It is not always happy or easy or fun and yet there is so much to be gained that the invitation to become a part of God's people is too good to pass by. We will suffer heartaches but we will also rejoice in the fond and sometimes amusing memories of life in the Family of Faith.

2

The Church Is Here To Stay

"He said to them, "But who do you say that I am?" Simon Peter answered, "You are the Messiah, the Son of the Living God." And Jesus answered him, "Blessed are you, Simon son of Jonah! For flesh and blood has not revealed this to you but my Father in heaven. And I tell you, you are Peter and on this rock I will build my Church and the gates of Hades will not prevail against it." (MATTHEW 16:15–18)

It was late on a Sunday afternoon when I returned home from a Church meeting and was met on my front porch by an unexpected visitor, a friend who like myself was heavily involved in the life and work of our denomination in Virginia. After explaining the reason for his visit, we began discussing the latest Church news of the day. The early 70's you may recall was a time when articles, books and even sermons were flying off the press about the demise of the Church and the irrelevance of faith in modern society. My friend remarked that, "They can make all the predictions of doom and gloom that they want, I believe in the Church and the Church is here to stay!"

Now, well into the 21st century we look back over those 40 years and realize that indeed it hasn't been an easy time for the Church, but look! The Church is still here. Today, among similar cries of irrelevance and attempts to conduct the funeral of the Church, those words still ring true— "The Church is here to stay." To know anything from history is to understand that the Church has always been on thin ice. There were times such as the evangelical surge of the late 19th and early 20th centuries, or the more gentle 1950's when the Church seemed to be held in higher esteem by the general public but the Church does not depend on public opinion for it's life, purpose and mission. The Church is here to stay because it is God's Church.

From the very beginning, Christians have been a people called and sent.—We are called to learn and understand the love and the ways of God. We are sent into the world of whatever era in which we live to share that understanding of God's ways and the experience of God's love. Are we always heard? No. Are we always appreciated? No. Should we give up? Never! It is still God's Church and as long as there are those who choose to fill its ranks, it will have life.

Times change, people change, the way we do things changes. The very face of daily living changes. That is why it is called life. Life is a living, moving, changing experience. That being said, there are some facts that are not altered. How often are we reminded that life consists of body, mind and spirit? But we don't always get the spirit part. Besides our need for food, sunshine, exercise and sleep for the body we recognize our need for mental exercise, emotional fulfillment and intellectual growth. But there is more—we are spiritual beings with a deep need to relate to something beyond ourselves. I accept the fact that there are many pathways to understanding and experiencing God. For me the way is through Jesus Christ. I find the Church to be where I can best express this understanding and share it with others. Whoever we are, there is something in life beyond ourselves and we must reach for it as well as share it. This is one reason that the Church is here to stay. Despite decline and change, there is the ever present hunger for meaning and hope. We are spiritual beings with a deep hunger for truth, meaning, assurance and faith. Matthew's Gospel tells of a moment when Jesus looked upon the crowds of people and he says,

> "When he saw the crowds, he had compassion on them because they were harassed and helpless, like sheep without a shepherd. Then he said to his disciples, "The harvest is plentiful, but the laborers are few therefore ask the Lord of the harvest to send out laborers into his harvest." (MATTHEW 9:36–38)

For those of us called to ministry within the Church, this is an urgent call to respond to a profound and very real need. It is a need that is as evident in the twenty first century as it was in the first. That call is to continue reaching and sharing. That means special preparation and education for the task at hand but it also means entering a world of challenges for which there is no formal preparation. Simply stated; There are things they can't teach you in seminary. The call to ministry comes without training wheels. In ministry, we are so often confronted with situations and surprises that could not possibly be anticipated by any text book. I say this with no intent to put down, belittle or minimize the importance of theological education for ministry. There is no substitute for Biblical knowledge, theological reflection, lessons learned from experienced teachers and knowledgable mentors. But there can be no formal preparation for many of the people, situations and events that will be encountered when one answers a call to become the pastor of a Church.

3

Thank God And Take Courage

"Then I heard the voice of the Lord saying, "Whom shall I send and who will go for us?" Then I said, "Here am I; send me." (ISAIAH 6:8)

On a slow news day the General Synod of the United Church of Christ passed a resolution which was considered by some to be controversial. The media was on it like lightning. So it was that as a pastor in that denomination, I was called by a local TV station and asked If they could interview me concerning the matter. I met the reporter and the camera crew in our Church sanctuary. As they were setting up for the five minute interview the reporter looked around at the worshipful surroundings and said to me, "You must have a nice peaceful job." Obviously he had not had much exposure to ministry or the day to day world in which real ministry functions. If there is an ivory tower involved somewhere, I have not discovered it.

To be sure there must be quiet times of meditation and prayer. There are the hours of writing and preparing but there are the hours and days spent being there for people going through both the joy of living and the hell of physical, mental and spiritual agony. Phyllis and I both grew up in loving homes among caring families. Not everybody has this blessing. Early on in our ministry, I discovered another world out there where families are torn apart, husbands and wives grow to hate each other and children suffer the consequences. Ministry has taken me to homes where suspicion and fear fill every corner, to jails where Sunday School graduates are spending time and to counseling sessions where I have heard stories that would curl the hair of any seasoned psychiatrist.

Each year at the annual congregational business meeting of the Church I would present as a part of my report, the number of visits made during the year in homes and hospitals. One year, I added to this category, a number for jail visits. A ripple of laughter went through the group. I looked at them and said, "Don't laugh, some of you go there." The messiness of life takes in Church member and non-member alike. It is a tough world out there and we are all in it together.

It was early fall in my third year of college when a knock came on the door of the classroom where I was more or less paying attention to the professor's lecture. The Dean of the college poked his head in the door and motioned to me saying, "I need to talk to you." Believe me, that was a scary moment. I followed him into the hallway and he motioned to an empty room and asked me to sit down. By now I was sure I must be in big trouble of some kind. He started to speak: "I was wondering if you would like to do some preaching." Without hesitation, I replied, "Sure," even though I had not turned twenty years of age. He then told me of a small Baptist Church in the country who had asked if the college had any available students who could fill their pulpit for a few Sundays.

Arriving for the evening service on a dark night and entering the sanctuary we were greeted by a deacon who introduced himself and handed me a hymnal. "Can I see your bulletin?" I said. His look assured me that bulletins were not a part of their vocabulary. "What is your order of service for tonight?" I inquired. He pointed to the hymnbook and said, "Anything you want to do." Here was a crash course in thinking fast and making quick decisions. But it all went well. I was invited back to preach the next Sunday morning.

Two weeks later, the deacons called me up front where they were counting the offering. "We would like you to be our preacher," they said handing me my pay for the evening and informing me of their monthly schedule. They had one service every Sunday,—two were morning services and two were in the evening and Prayer Meeting every Wednesday.

It was there in Cornerstone Baptist Church that I conducted my first funeral. It was the first funeral I ever attended. It was also here that I did my first baptisms which were by immersion and included some people who weighed twice as much as I did.

I continued to be their pastor for two more years until I had finished college, married Phyllis and headed for Rochester New York, Colgate Rochester Divinity School and the Methodist congregation I would serve for the next three years. There, in Lake Avenue Methodist Church I learned how to baptize infants and how much that experience means to a family. Here also was where I was called to the hospital at 7 A.M. on a winter morning to baptize a child born the night before with little chance of surviving long enough to go home. Of course the child did not know the difference but the comfort brought to the parents was immeasurable. My first weddings were conducted here also. As I made visits to people in all conditions of life, usually the sick and shut in, I began to understand what is meant by the ministry of presence.

In those first two pastorates, I learned more about being a pastor than all the college or seminary courses I took could ever teach me. By that I do not mean to belittle any of the things I gained in formal education but as the old saying goes, "Experience is the best teacher." Unlike learning to ride a bicycle, there are no training wheels for your first pastorate. Just watch, listen, learn, pray and hang on!

In the Book of Acts, we find Paul headed toward Rome and an uncertain future. He is met on the way by friends who have come to meet him. The writer says,

"On seeing them, Paul thanked God and took courage."

That describes the approach we need to meet many of the unknown or uncertain experiences we face in ministry. All we can do is, "Thank God and take courage." No classroom lesson can prepare you for the morning you discover a suicide victim and then drive to the school to tell his young children what happened. No textbook can prepare you to help the person who comes to your office and has a meltdown over a failed marriage. Nobody prepares you in advance for dealing with an irate, unreasonable and cantankerous Church officer intent on giving you trouble. Nobody tells you what to say to the parents of a stillborn child. No teacher can prepare you for the moment a really earnest seven year old stops you in the Church hallway and asks in earnest expectation, "Where's God?"

On the other hand, what class or textbook prepares you for the ring bearer who loses his lunch during the wedding ceremony? As there are tears and heartaches and difficult situations, there are also joys and laughter. No one can describe the warmth and appreciation of those who are truly helped by your ministry and presence, or the satisfaction of knowing you have helped someone along life's journey. Nobody can teach those things. They come without preparation. Ministry happens just as life happens. "Thank God and take courage."

4

Just Call Me Pastor

"In the presence of God and Christ Jesus, who is to judge the living and the dead, and in view of his appearing and his kingdom, I solemnly urge you, proclaim the message; be persistent whether the time is favorable or unfavorable; convince, rebuke and encourage, with the utmost patience in teaching." (II TIMOTHY 4:1–2)

While I was in my second pastorate, I went shopping for a used car. As I looked around the lot a salesman approached me and introduced himself. I told him my name and he asked where I worked. I explained that I was Pastor of a Church in the city. Somewhat taken aback, he said, "Oh, what should I call you? Your Reverence?" "Dave would be fine" I explained. In some communities, especially rural ones it is customary to refer to the minister as "Preacher." While that is appropriate, I prefer to be called "Pastor." Preaching is of utmost importance to me and involves hours of careful preparation. I love to preach, I believe in preaching, however, let me emphasize that the day to day life of ministry must be pastoral or it is irrelevant. You can preach, lead, serve on denominational boards, all of which I have done but to be truly a minister of Jesus Christ is to exercise daily pastoral care. The needs and opportunities are never ending.

Pastoral duties run from the routine, to eye opening experiences and sometimes to the bizarre. As for an eye opener, I learned early on that not everyone grew up with the blessing of a loving nurturing family as I had. Early one morning, I was called to a home where the mother had taken off in the night with her new boy friend, leaving her husband, who was not prepared for this with two young school age children. As he explained to me what had happened the children cried in their confusion. There was little or no food in the house and the man didn't even drive or own a car. Caring Church members and a social worker addressed the immediate needs but how does one answer the questions or deal with the sense of abandonment in those children? Somehow you find a way to do it and pray that you did it right.

Then there was the cold winter morning when the phone rang at 7:30 just as we were leaving the house. The frantic voice on the other end said, "I just found my husband in the car in the garage with the motor running. I am not sure he is alive." Phyllis volunteered to take the bus to work while I rushed to the scene of distress. Quickly I entered the garage where the man lay on the front seat of a new car. I pushed him over so I could get beneath the wheel and backed out of the garage then called the ambulance. He appeared to me to be dead and most likely it was suicide. As the paramedics frantically worked on him his two small sons got on the school bus. In a few moments the paramedics delivered the expected news. He was gone. Now it was my job to go to the school where I explained the situation to the Principal. He called the boys to the office and gave us a private room where in the most understanding terms I could, told them their Father was dead. You might say that it is all in a day's work, but those are days you never forget and hope they don't occur again.—But they will.

At times the pastoral experience can border on the bizarre. A Deacon in the Church was falsely accused and fired from his job. It happened on the same day that his wife was diagnosed with cancer. It is hard to imagine the crushing weight on his shoulders at that time. Nevertheless he became the subject of a high profile jury trial. I for one believed in him and even though I didn't have first hand knowledge of the case, I could comfortably vouch for his character. I believe that my character witness for him in court was instrumental in acquitting him of all charges and being restored to his job. What a joy it was to be invited to a celebration which he held for all who had helped him and stood by him through this difficult time.

Most of all, the pastoral presence is seen in the hospital visits, the weddings, the funerals and the ongoing counseling sessions. These are all a sacred trust and define the purpose of our day to day function in ministry. The trust invested by those we serve allows us into the most sacred and touching experiences and occasions of their lives. At times of grief and joy alike we are there. These occasions along with the opportunities to speak on Christ's behalf call to mind again the command given to Moses as he stood in the presence of God,

> *"Remove the sandals from your feet for the place on which you are standing is Holy Ground."* (EXODUS 3:5)

One day I stood in reverent silence in a hospital room with a Church member and friend and his young adult children as the life support systems were removed from their wife and mother. No one said anything as for the next twenty minutes she slipped quietly into the presence of our Lord. My presence there and in the days that followed was a comfort to them. Their trust was a sacred gift to me.

To be pastor is to share in the tragedies, sadness and the celebrations, light hearted moments and joys of life. To be invited in is an act of faith and trust not to be taken lightly. Ministry is never a job or a career. It is a Calling. It can not be adjusted to a time clock or a normal schedule. Often ministry happens. The emergencies that send a pastor to visit a hospital at midnight, the late night calls from someone who needs to talk, the happenings in human life are not scheduled on a calendar or a clock. My experience has been that even in "retirement", I am called upon for hospital visits, counseling and denominational responsibilities. I embrace these as a fulfillment of what God called me long ago to be and to do and I am grateful for the strength and energy to be of service to God's people and God's Church.

Ministry is not only a Calling. It is an attitude. No one is entitled to do ministry—we are entrusted with it. As the Apostle Paul reminds us,

> *"But we have this treasure in clay jars so that, it may be made clear that this extraordinary power belongs to God and does not come from us."* (II CORINTHIANS 4:7)

5

Guess What Happened In Church Today

"O come, let us worship and bow down, let us kneel before the Lord our maker! For he is our God and we are the people of his pasture and the sheep of his hand." (PSALM 95:6–7)

Unfortunately and yet fortunately, most Sunday Morning Worship Services do not linger long in memory. The hope is that even though the actual occasion may be soon obscured by the ongoing events of daily life, somehow something of value was gained. There may have been a respite from an otherwise hectic week. Comfort could be found in the singing and prayers or some word of meaningful insight gained from the Pastor's Message. Surely we find the worship experience meaningful or helpful or we would not continue to participate.

Scripture stands the test of time because it is always relevant. Among the stories, legends and history we realize who we are—that is, God's people and we discover what we are here for as Christ's disciples. Here we find that life has real meaning and consists of more than the physical and material features of daily life. We are also spiritual beings and we are the creation of a divine parent. More than random events, life has purpose. Amidst chaos there can be order and peace of heart and mind. All of this is reinforced in the experience of worship. It is in worship that we do more than claim to have faith. Here is a means of expressing that faith with the community of others who share in it's promises and hope. Familiar hymns and old stories combine with fresh insights to give us encouragement and hope in a world that is often skeptical and bleak. Often it is just being in worship and acknowledging the presence of God with others who like ourselves are seeking answers that we find renewal and a sense of meaning. In the United Church of Christ we like to say, "God is still speaking." The ongoing conversation between God and ourselves can happen anywhere we may be but surely worship gives us a time dedicated to this wonderful truth. When we come with expectancy, we are rarely disappointed.

A Psalm speaks to us saying, *"Be still and know that I am God…"* Be still and know—The practice of worship affords us that opportunity. Life can be joyous or difficult, hectic or peaceful but know this, life is full of surprises. As we make preparation in every other area of our experience, we must also be prepared and aware spiritually and inwardly. Our encounter with the divine is best understood and appreciated if it is a familiar and ongoing experience rather than an occasional or emergency happening. Those who gave us beautiful Psalms and memorable scripture verses, didn't sit around and make it all up. They were speaking from their life's experience and blessing us with a look at what the presence of God can be in our daily lives.

Like any other public event, there are stories and unusual happenings to come from our time gathered as God's people. Where there are people gathered together there will be emergencies, there will be humor, there will sometimes be strange happenings. No manner of event is immune from this possibility. One Sunday the message was just concluded and we stood to sing the Communion hymn when there was a loud crash in the choir loft. I rushed over to see Fred lying on the floor and from his appearance I knew he had to be dead. A pharmacist and a nurse in the congregation rushed to his side while I asked someone to call 911. I then dismissed the crowd, asking them to leave quietly and with a prayer for Fred. He was rushed to the hospital while I saw to the details at the Church. A couple hours later when I arrived at the hospital there was Fred, sitting up in bed and looking well. He had given us all a scare but two weeks later he was in his usual place in the back row of the choir.

Then there was the Spring Sunday Morning when it was too warm for heat and not hot enough for air conditioning but cool enough that all the doors and windows were tightly closed. Stuffy air can affect some people adversely and so it was that as the pastoral prayer began a small boy sitting with his Grandmother began to lose his breakfast on the floor. The episode continued on for a seeming eternity and for some reason it struck me funny. Then a lady got up and left, and that made it seem even funnier. The Grandmother made no move to take him out while surrounding worshippers suffered quietly. To give him a chance to finish or leave, I continued slowly praying hoping the matter would resolve soon while heads were bowed. It was a very, very long prayer. Finally, Grandma got up, left the boy there then reappeared with a mop and a towel and took care of things right there before taking the child home. As for the content of the sermon that day, I am sure no one remembers.

Children's sermons are more important than they appear to most adults. Surely the content is not that profound or memorable but to recognize the little ones in our midst and include them will have a lasting effect on their life and faith. It is also humorous and possibly dangerous. I always like to get the kids to talk and tell a little about their life and experience and to share what is important to them. Sometimes they tell more than their parents want them to. I have actually known one family who would go home after Sunday School on a week that they were afraid what little Mary might tell. Then there was the Sunday after Christmas when I gathered the children around and spoke to them of the three wise men. Some of them were able to answer when I asked, "What were the gifts the wise men brought to the Baby Jesus?" "That's right" I said, "and I have here a sample of these three gifts, gold, frankincense and myrrh. Let me pass them around and you can hold them in your hand and look at them." As I passed the myrrh, little Joey popped it straight into his mouth. I immediately stuck my finger in his mouth and popped it out and said, " I think you better let me hold these gifts and you can just look at them. One morning when the little ones had gathered on the front row for their part of the service, an angel faced little girl started things off by announcing to me, "I brought a dime for the offering but I lost it in the toilet." How do you top that one?

Baptism by immersion is the practice of the Christian Church (Disciples of Christ) where most of my ministry has taken place. While it is a solemn, reverent and respected practice the opportunities for mishaps, disruption and humor are ever present. There was the young lady who thought she was supposed to go under the water three times instead of once who gave me a scare. There was the lady who stepped into the water and cried out, "It's cold" and then there was Robby. Robby was slightly young for believer's baptism but he had attended the Pastor's Class and talked it over with his parents and so on Sunday he joined the others who were being baptized. When he got into the baptistery he began laughing and when I immersed him under the water he began kicking and blowing. Water was bubbling and spraying everywhere. Some later suggested that Robbie should wait and be baptized again but that never happened. Instead, about twenty years later when we were invited back to that Church for a special occasion, we were greeted by Robbie, a young family man and respected leader in the Church.

Things are not always as they appear. It was on a beautiful Spring Sunday in Lent when I spoke to the worshippers about meaningful sacrifice. I pointed out that to give up soda or candy or smoking for Lent was trivial and meaningless. What if during this season we became more mindful of human need and reached out to others around us? I pointed out that most of us were fortunate and I said, "All of us will leave here this morning assured that we will eat whether it be at home or a restaurant." As I stood at the door to greet the departing worshippers there were the usual comments, "See you next Sunday." "Good sermon, Pastor," "How are you today?" and then came a well dressed working mother, an active Church worker and her three well dressed young sons. The first thing she said to me was, "No, I don't know where or if we will eat today. When we left the house my husband was in a drunken rage and had been threatening us. He slammed the door behind us and yelled at us not to come back." There is more to the story than that but surely the lesson here is, don't judge by appearances or assume that everyone is as fortunate as you are. Behind many an expensive suit beats a broken heart and within the facade of many a beautiful suburban home there is strife and pain. The old saying is surely true that says, "There is a broken heart in every pew." The Church must be a caring place even when we aren't always aware of who it is we should be caring about.

Often when the service is over and people are leaving worship you hear their stories, especially the reason they didn't make it last week. There are the reasons like, oversleeping, had to work, sick, out of town. Whenever the sentence begins with, "I didn't want to get too far from the bathroom," you can be sure that what follows will be far more information than you need. It happens a lot.

Present on any given Sunday will be some who don't exactly hear things as they are meant to be. One day my message was based on a New Testament character named Demas. Demas was a helper of Paul and as you read Paul's letters you can trace his faith from active and enthusiastic to finally total desertion. I used that as an example of how some modern Christians begin well and then fade away in time. As I greeted the folks at the door, one faithful old lady exclaimed, *"I sure hope I ain't one of them demons!"*

The next time someone comes home from worship and says, "Guess what happened in Church today," don't be surprised, anything can happen.

6

Good News!

"But how are they to call on one in whom they have not believed? And how are they to believe in one of whom they have never heard? And how are they to hear without someone to proclaim him? And how are they to proclaim him unless they are sent? As it is written, 'How beautiful are the feet of those who bring good news!" (ROMANS 10:14–15)

The first image that comes to mind when we speak of ministry is that of preacher. Although it is but part of the high calling, it's importance is at the forefront. On any given Sunday, those who assemble for worship are there for many reasons and with different attitudes. Some are actually there with anticipation expecting to be nourished in mind and soul. What an awesome responsibility to be the one to whom they look with hunger and expectation.

Effective and meaningful preaching is impossible without study, discipline, a willingness to be constantly observing and learning. It is also dependent on prayer and faith. I have shelves of books including the works of most of the great pulpit voices of the 20th century. However, the effectiveness of those sermons can not be measured by how well they read or the number of books they sell but in the lives of the original hearers. For this there is no graph, scale or statistic. What gems of wisdom, hope, faith or positive assurance are proclaimed depends partially on the hearers but mostly on the sincere, informed faith of the speaker. Informed faith and effective communication are no accident. One ministerial colleague I knew along the way once stated that he preached only because it was part of his job and he was expected to. The comments I heard from his congregation truly supported that statement. Effective preaching includes the burning desire to proclaim the Good News. The prophet Jeremiah spoke of the fire shut up in his bones. Paul said, *"Woe is me if I preach not the Gospel."* One Saturday during my student years, my seminary advisor spoke with me about my preaching assignment for the next day. He said, "You and the Lord have something important to say tomorrow." That is something to remember. Preaching is no casual event, no mere entertainment. It is serious business and demands our best.

Effective preaching begins with the Bible and passes through today's news and whatever is going on in the life experience of the listeners. For me, preaching is applying faith to daily experience that speaks to individual lives and the condition of society at the moment. Sermons involve humor, stories, down-to-earth experience, Biblical interpretation and understanding and engaging oratory but these are just some of the tools for presenting the message and making it clear. Besides beginning with the Bible, most messages must take into account the daily newspaper. Not that it necessarily needs to be quoted but the preacher who is unaware of what is going on in the world on any given day probably has little to say of any relevance.

It has been said that the best advice for public speaking is, "stand up, speak up and shut up." That is good advice. Lengthy sermons are just that—lengthy. Learn to make a point in a few words. The less reading of the manuscript, the better. My method is to prepare carefully and write out a full manuscript. Then before preaching, I familiarize myself with the message by reading it over several times. Then I leave it home on my desk and go preach it. If something gets left out or something else gets added, so be it. Too much reading of the manuscript can be deadly. If I can't remember what I have to say, why should anyone else? In all honesty, any preacher appreciates the time when the worshippers are leaving the service with such comments as, "Good message," "I appreciated the sermon, " enjoyed the message," but perhaps the best comment we could hear is, "I was really helped by what you said." Cherish that one for when you hear it, you will know that you have done your job well. Preaching demands preparation, discipline, study, practical knowledge and prayer. Never underestimate the importance of preaching. The prophets took it seriously. Jesus was a preacher. Jesus sends us out into the world to be his witnesses.

However, it is here that we must be reminded that Worship and preaching is a two way street. No matter how eloquent the sermon or uplifting the hymns and music, no matter how great the fellowship, the worshipper must be open to receive the Spirit of God. Those who come expecting little, will receive little and those who open their hearts and minds with anticipation will be truly blessed. In the course of his letter to the Romans, Paul exclaims,

> *"O the depth of the riches and wisdom and knowledge of God! How unsearchable are his judgments and how inscrutable his ways! For who has known the mind of the Lord or who has been his counselor? Or who has given a gift to him to receive a gift in return? For from him and through him and to him are all things. To him be glory forever. Amen."* (ROMANS 11:33–35)

This is an eloquent reminder of the unlimited depth of God's love, insights and the power of God's presence among us. We can not begin to exhaust the resources of God which are constantly available to us. This speaks also to the worship experience. Who knows the power, wisdom and assurance that can pour into our lives when we are truly open to the Spirit of God. Too often many present in worship do not move from the social level of Church life to the spiritual heights that we are invited to enter in the community of faith.

In the fourth chapter, John's Gospel tells of Jesus' encounter with a man who was unable to walk and who had come to the healing waters of the Pool of Siloam for thirty eight years. To this man, Jesus asked a searching question, "Do you want to be healed?" In other words, "What is your excuse?" When the man said that he really wanted to be healed, Jesus said, "Rise, take up your pallet and walk."

Jesus' question to this man is important for all of us. "Do you want to be healed?" Or broadened to meet our needs, do we really want to encounter God's Spirit? Are we willing to be challenged or risk a change of attitude or be called to compassion and service? Or do we close our hearts and minds to these possibilities and miss the Spirit when the Spirit would come to us. Something to think about as we participate in the Worship of the Church.

7

I Was Sick And You Visited Me

"...I was sick and you took care of me, I was in prison and you visited me..." (MATTHEW 25:36)

To be a pastor is to spend countless hours in hospitals and by sick beds. When the faithful can not come to the Church, the Church must come to the faithful. There is no way to understate the importance of this fact. We pastors are not miracle working healers as was reported of Jesus. We are however, healers by our presence and caring. I believe strongly not only by faith but by experience that prayer and pastoral care factor into the healing process and can indeed help its progress. From early on, I have made it a priority to visit the sick including many years in a volunteer hospital chaplaincy program. What is encountered here is everything from the humorous to the tragic.

I can only recall one occasion when my hospital visit was not appreciated. I was making my volunteer chaplain rounds when I stopped by the room of a lady who had just been admitted. I introduced myself and inquired if she would like me to inform her pastor that she was here. She rose up and looked at me and very plainly stated that her pastor was one of the well known T V evangelists of the day.

I turned and left. What I wanted to say was, "Let me know when that man visits you."

On the other hand there was the young couple who had some Pentecostal beliefs who asked me to go to the hospital and anoint their very sick child and have prayer. I am not big on anointing but I understand that it is meaningful to some and it is scriptural. I visited the child early one morning and performed this ministry. Later the delighted couple informed me that the child's fever broke that day and she was much better that night. I claim no credit for this but if anything I did was of help, that is the pastor's role.

Soon after a new state of the art medical facility was built in a community near our Church, I visited a member who was undergoing tests. The new hospital had been declared a total non smoking zone and signs to that effect were everywhere. As I visited with my friend, he pulled a cigarette from his pocket and proceeded to light it, informing me that if he was having to pay $1,000.00 a day for the room he would do as he pleased. Nobody tried to stop him.

A Church member who was a retired educator with a PhD. was hospitalized for a heart condition. He was in his 80's and scheduled for open heart surgery. As we talked he said to me, "You know, I have lived a long time and had a good life. I think I will pass on the surgery and get along as best I can in the days I have left." The next morning when I came to his room, he was being prepped for surgery. In the night he had witnessed his room mate die of heart failure and decided he better go ahead with the operation. It was successful.

There are times when I believe that in spite of whatever good I may have done or what ever difference was made, it was I who was blessed the most by the belief that I had made an effort to help and had made a difference in someone's life for a day or a lifetime. Sometimes it is more important to spend a few hours with an anxious family in a waiting room as it is to be by a patient's bedside. The expression, "ministry of presence" is much more than that, it is a proven fact.

Not every ending is happy and that is another reason why ministry to the sick is so important. An active leader in our Church passed away one July after a long illness. Her husband who had also become active in the Church suffered profound grief but appeared to be in good health. He remained active until 5 months later when he was hospitalized for slight pneumonia. He appeared to be recovering nicely when I visited him one morning but he said to me, "I have come here to die." "No" I said, "You are going to be OK." In less than a week he was dead. There is something to be said for the will to live and the power we have over our own well being. Surely the decision as to our leaving this world is not entirely ours but I have to believe that my friend did not recover because he did not want to.

As pastors our expertise and role is not medicine. It is to bring the healing presence of the God we represent by our faith and caring. It is through prayer and caring that we reach into a person's life and make a difference. It is not our business to offer remedies or ask a lot of questions. I have seen pastors ask questions of a patient that were none of their business. I watched one day in a hospital room as a fellow pastor asked a doctor many questions about a parishioner's illness and tried comically to use medical terms he thought would impress the doctor. If a doctor comes in during your pastoral visit, your job is to leave the room until the doctor is finished. We are not doctors. Let us remember our role. It is important in it's own right.

Sometimes there is more life underneath the weak smile and tired countenance of a patient than we realize. I had visited an outspoken and strong willed lady during her illness at home, later a nursing home and then in the hospital. One day she lay there while I did most of the talking. I don't recall what the subject was but I made the comment, "That's what the old people said but what did they know?" Immediately she sat up straight, looked me in the eye, shook her finger and said, "A hell of a lot!" Don't ever assume that in any circumstances your words are taken lightly.

There are so many visits with the sick in homes, nursing homes and hospitals through the years, that it is impossible to remember them all. Those that are especially humorous, eventful or sad stand out in memory. The important point is to understand that whether or not these visits seem routine, they are more important than we realize at the time. Jesus placed his hand on the sick child and she got up out of her sick bed. He spoke to the crippled man on the stretcher and he got up and walked. He went where no one else would go and placed his hand on the lepers and they were made whole. As his representatives in the world of today we can not and must not make any such claims for ourselves. Nevertheless we are called to be a part of the healing process. Jesus came as one who cared. Jesus sends us to many places as those who care. If we don't care we shouldn't go there. When we read the New Testament accounts of Jesus' healing someone they are often preceded with the words, "He took pity," or "He had compassion on them." To bring the gift of prayer and comfort is important and it is the caring that validates our gifts of faith and presence.

8

Hard Luck On The Move

"Do not neglect to show hospitality to strangers for by doing that, some have entertained angels without knowing it." (Hebrews 13:2)

If you have never answered the knock on your door and found a stranger asking for help, chances are you have not been a pastor for long. It will happen and it will probably happen many times. There is a segment of the population that stays on the move or stays in hard luck. I am no fan of country music but I will have to say that all the themes of heartache, bad luck and being down - and - out are true to life. I will also have to say that after enough stories about dead grandmothers, family fights where people have been tossed out, lost wallets, cross-country trips to seek a job, mothers in surgery, etc. etc. one tends to grow skeptical and cynical. All of the above are recurring themes among those likely to knock on your door at any time of day or night. I know that I have encountered my share of con artists, lazy slackers and fugitives from justice. However the task of judgment is not always ours. The call to help is.

One of the first experiences with strangers came while we were still in my student pastorate in Seminary. An older man in a raincoat and wearing a beard came to the door on a rainy evening and asked for money for a meal. We gave him a small amount and told him where the local restaurants were located. Later, as we walked to the Church on our way to a meeting we saw him eating in a pizza shop. Phyllis, being the ever considerate and compassionate one, insisted that we go in and see if he was alright. He looked at us with grateful eyes, never mentioning the food but profusely thanking us for caring enough to look in on him. "No one ever did that before," he said.

Several years later, I was called to Northern Virginia to a rather large Church in a not so large town. Being located by two major highways, our town had many visitors stopping in, and asking for help. One feature of that community was a special fund supported by the four larger Churches. The funds were administered by an officer of a local bank and allocated by the pastors of the participating Churches. The original idea was to help local families in hard circumstances with small daily needs. This, it did very well but many times we called upon the funds for travelers with bad luck. I recall the man who stopped by on Thanksgiving Day as we were finishing our meal. We brought him in and gave him a big plate of food before taking him to a nearby city to a shelter. But there were many others who stretched both patience and credibility.

One January afternoon an old Buick packed full of people pulled up. A loud talking woman came to the door and announced that there were six people in the car and they needed food and gas. Keep in mind that this was January but her story was that they were traveling from Tampa, Florida to Syracuse, New York to get jobs in a drive - in restaurant. I was ready for that one. I just said, "I am from that area and I happen to know that drive in restaurants don't stay open there this time of year."

A man wearing a suit and carrying a briefcase appeared one day claiming that he was starting work at the local newspaper but he needed some money until he got paid. To impress me he claimed to be a member of a Disciples of Christ Church in Kentucky. I had already been warned of this man by the Lutheran pastor. The man had told him he belonged to a Lutheran Church in New York. When I told him I was wise to his story, he indignantly shouted, "I hope your Master will remember this!"

When a call came one night from a local gas station, I went to see what I could do. I went in and they told me which car the man was driving. He said he had no money for gas. He was driving a Cadillac! We gave him enough gas to get him out of town. On another evening, at another gas station the driver needing fuel asked for toll money for the Pennsylvania Turnpike. He was headed home to Indiana. I explained to him that he did not have to go via the Turnpike. I handed him a road map and pointed out another route. He was totally disinterested in my suggestions.

On a cool June evening a man claiming to be from a town in the southern part of the state, stopped by asking if I had a jacket he could wear. I went to the attic and found one. Later, I learned that he went next to the Presbyterian Church asking for a jacket and it had to be a specific type and color. Who said, "Beggars can't be choosers"?

A hippie type couple came to my office one day, complete with guitar, saying that they were traveling and singing Gospel music when they could gather an audience. Today however, they were down on their luck and needed food, money and a place to stay. I was quite suspicious of them but I asked them to sit down while I called a friend in the next community who had connections to a group that might help them. For some reason they took offense that I would call someone else in and they stormed out loudly yelling about the "system" and people like me who were a part of it.

The Churches of our community also had an understanding with some local restaurants. We could send someone there who needed a meal and they would bill us for it. One morning, a man who needed food came to one of the other Churches in the community seeking help. Apparently he was sent to one of these restaurants. Later I received a call from someone at the restaurant. They couldn't get in touch with the pastor who sent him there; could I help them? This man had eaten three pancake breakfasts and numerous cups of coffee. How much more should they give him? I said, "I think he has had enough." They said, "He says he isn't finished yet." I replied, "He is now."

Perhaps the best story is what happened one day when I was out of town. As Phyllis watched from the window, an old Chevy pulled up in front of the house. The driver got out, took a jack from the trunk and pretended to jack up a rear wheel. Phyllis could see that there were no flat tires on the car. The man came and rang the doorbell and when asked what he wanted, he tried to push his way in saying that he needed money for a tire. As she politely refused and sent the man on his way, she turned to see our six year old son coming down the stairs armed with his authentic looking Johnny Eagle, toy rifle, loaded with plastic bullets and ready to defend his mother from any dangerous characters!

I once read an article in a Minister's journal by a pastor in a distant state describing his experiences and the experiences of others with those who come seeking help. It was amazing how many of his accounts were exactly like what I have experienced over time. Jesus reminded his disciples that the opportunity to help the poor was always with them. It still is. In the end, how can we judge? Well meaning people make bad decisions. Others seem prone to bad judgment and hard luck. We can only reach out and help and hope and pray that we have done well and that someone was truly helped along the way.

9

Beyond The Flock

"And I have other sheep that do not belong to this fold;
I must bring them also, and they will listen to my voice."
(JOHN 10:16)

As I have said before, if there is an ivory tower involved in ministry, I haven't found it. Nor am I looking for it. It is very clear that Jesus spent most of his time where there was need. If he wasn't teaching, he was healing, helping, giving of himself. To be sure, he sought times of solace, rest, meditation and prayer. Never be deceived into thinking you can survive long without these. But when he was refreshed and renewed he returned to life with all of it's joys, needs and difficulties.

Just as there are no ivory towers, we realize also that ministry can not just take place within the walls of a Church building or be restricted to the members of one congregation. To truly minister is to be out in the community among all kinds of people and needs. The Church and pastor totally wrapped up in their own concerns with no vision for the community is destined for failure. To truly minister is to go out into the community. More often than you may realize, the community will come to you.

One Sunday evening a young man appeared at the door practically dragging a poor girl by the arm. He demanded that I tell her that she was wrong and he was right. Still young and inexperienced myself, I couldn't really see where this was going but I invited them in and asked them to have a seat. The man was quick to tell his version of the dispute they were having, the details of which I have long since forgotten. I realized something that I would experience many times in such situations that there are times when listening is important but not enough. Sometimes you have to do the talking. Since I probably would not see these people again, I gave the young man a talk in no uncertain terms about the fact that marriage and relationships are mutual. He was not the boss, he was one half of a partnership. I don't know if it worked but I hope it helped. I am sure I did the right thing.

In another community, the Church was located within sight of a high school. On occasion a student would stop by my office with a spiritual concern. Sometimes they were sent to me by a teacher who felt the student's question was beyond their expertise. On more than one occasion, questions had been raised about such issues as Satanism or ouigi boards. Sometimes there were problems at home. Always it was important to listen to the concern and give what guidance I could.

Ecumenicity is important no matter how large your own congregation or how great your responsibilities. In all of the communities where I served there was collegiality, communication and cooperation among clergy and churches. As varied expressions of Christian practice we all have something to share and a common interest in faith and service. Moreover we can always be prepared to help each other. Shared Worship on special occasions brings the communities of faith together. Some results of ecumencical cooperation have included a food pantry for those in need and a bowling league that involved teens to 70's. Helpful and wholesome activities are an expression of faith and good will. A spirit of trust and friendship can also be a fruit of a wider community of faith.

I believe that every local pastor who benefits from standing in a denomination should to some degree participate in the work of that denomination in the region and beyond. All through my ministry it has been a privilege to hold positions of leadership and committee membership that advance the common life of the wider body whose principles we embrace. Serving on committees and as Moderator of a region have been demanding but productive. To this day I am pleased to fulfill responsibilities in each of the denominations where I hold standing. The wider church benefits from such participation and the local congregation is drawn in to the ministries that extend beyond their front door.

Not everyone would have the same experience or opportunities that I have had, but for several years I had the opportunity to serve in political office. People will tell you now as they said then, it is a recipe for disaster for a pastor to enter politics. Perhaps so, but I did it anyway when an opening came in our city council. I ran in spite of some criticism and won by a narrow margin. I enjoyed the experience and ran for two successive terms winning by a high margin. There were some tight ropes to walk, especially when we had to fire a town employee who was an Elder in the Church. There were zoning controversies also. But there was also the opportunity to invite a community college to the area, to address safety concerns and seek to improve life for all in the community. It was a personal risk but it was worthwhile. Ministry, after all, is not for the faint of heart.

As I mentioned before, often the community will come to you. It was 3 A.M. when the phone rang on a Sunday morning. It happened to be January 6th, the Day of Epiphany. If epiphany means a revealing or an eye opening experience, this was one. When I answered the phone, the voice on the other end informed me of who he was. It was the Council Chair of one of the other local churches. Their parsonage was next door to ours. My caller informed me that Pastor Joe was drinking heavily and was calling people up and cursing them out. His family was away. He was alone at home. My caller said, "Somebody has to go in there and help him, could you go with me?" I told him I would meet him there. As we entered the unlocked front door we could hear Pastor Joe upstairs yelling on the phone. There we found him, sitting on the side of the bed in his underwear on the phone, cursing out a pastor in a neighboring town. He had already called several officers of his church and drunkenly informed them of his opinions on how they were doing their jobs. When he hung up the phone, he started in on us with his complaints of everything that was wrong. There had indeed been problems in the Church but this seemed hardly the way to address them. With his rage intensifying, he grabbed up his clothes, including his clerical collar and flung them across the room. We tried to get him calmed down. I will never forget the hurt in his eyes at that moment. Clearly, this was a totally broken man. By 6 A.M. we had him sitting at his kitchen table and hopefully settling down although it was evident that he was in no shape to conduct worship that day. A retired chaplain who was a member of that church came into the room and Pastor Joe started in again as he sidled over to a cabinet which contained a gallon of whiskey. He poured himself a glass, took a sip, then threw it across the room between us where it hit a radiator and smashed. In the meantime, members of the church council, afraid to come in, went next door to our house and gathered in the living room. As they met deciding what to do next, Phyllis served them coffee and offered them cake. By 7:30 A.M. Pastor Joe had passed out, was loaded on an ambulance and sent to the lock ward at the hospital. In the days and weeks that followed, I found myself ministering to him, his family and members of his congregation. It was I who drove him to the airport one day to fly to a rehab center several states away. Pastor Joe made somewhat of a recovery and we were able to find him a low stress job where he worked for several years.

    Just a curious footnote to the above—Exactly one year later, January 6th, I left the Church office and walked across the street to go home for dinner. As I walked into the house, Phyllis said, "Don't take off your coat." "Why?" I said. She replied, "It's Epiphany isn't it?..A call came in from the apartment house up the road and one of our members has been drinking all week end. They want you to come. When I got there, the lady was on a stretcher on her way to the hospital. "She looked at me and with a big smile waved and said "Hi Rev. Derby good to see you, I'll be coming to Church" then fell back onto the gurney to resume her journey.

Epiphany may be a special holy day on the liturgical calendar but one thing I know. It will always be remembered on my calendar.

I would not label myself as a pacifist but I am vehemently opposed to war. War is the ultimate madness in human affairs and the result of the failure of reason and the nobler qualities of life. But war is also a reality. As this is being written America is still embroiled in the failing conflicts in Iraq and Afghanistan both of which rank up there with Vietnam in their futility and senseless loss. One Sunday morning a young man I had not met before came to worship. He had been invited by a neighbor who was aware of his inner conflict. At the close of worship he asked if he could speak with me in private. I took him into my office. His problem was that he was scheduled to leave home and join the military soon. However, he was increasingly troubled at the prospect of having to kill other human beings. On a couple of occasions in the past, I had suggested the idea of conscientious objection. In this case, the young man had enlisted and was committed to go. What was there to offer him except to say that the occasion might not arise? Perhaps there were areas of service where he could avoid this. In any case, he would have to take each occasion and decision as it arose and seek to live as best he could in a difficult time. These are the difficult and sometimes no-win situations that young people in our world face today. There are no clichés or easy answers for them. We seek not only the peace that signals the end of war, we seek the peace of God within ourselves.

10

Whom God Has Joined Together...

"On the third day there was a wedding in Cana of Galilee, and the mother of Jesus was there: Jesus and his disciples had also been invited to the wedding." (JOHN 2:1–2)

Among the challenging aspects of pastoral ministry is the conduct of weddings. These usually joyous occasions can range from the simple and dignified to the disastrous. Of course it is the disastrous ones that stand out in memory. Many funny things can happen at any wedding. Depending on the ingredients residing in any given family, a wedding can be a recipe for family fights, exploding tempers, confusion, and sometimes pure disrespect for the religious and the sacred.

I can easily recall my first wedding as the officiating pastor. The couple were both widowed and were great grandparents. Before the ceremony which went very smoothly, the groom had to be reminded to remove his winter boots and take his heart medicine. Not long after that, there was the wedding in the Church that involved a twin sister. The twins names were Elaine and Eileen. It was

Elaine who was getting married but it was Eileen's name that I called during the ceremony.

Late one night, I had just set the trash can on the curb for pick up the next morning. Before I turned the porch light off, Phyllis said, "Who are all these people in motorcycle jackets coming up the street?" I looked and said, "Don't look now but they are coming here." And so, I performed a wedding ceremony for the 16 year old bride and 24 year old groom in the living room in front of the TV.

It is said that people cry at weddings. Sometimes they do. The mother of the bride is too busy giving orders to cry. It is the father who is most likely to cry when his little girl, no matter how old she may be gets to the altar. As for the bridegrooms, these guys are very often in a daze. One evening when it was almost time for the ceremony to begin, the groom was missing. I went looking. He was wandering around the sanctuary, not fully dressed and talking to the guests as they arrived. We got that straightened out in a hurry. Then there was the high society wedding. This guy had to have everything just so, even to arriving with a police escort. He was a cool cat or so he thought. During the ceremony which involved enough attendants to form an army, it became very warm in the Church. It was time to place the ring on her finger. He tried but the finger must have been swollen or too warm. Finally he said in a loud voice, "I can't get the damn thing on!" Whatever else remained of that memorable day, that was tops.

One bride came from a broken home. I was not familiar with the family but there had been a bitter divorce between the bride's parents. So strong were the feelings, that family members came to me before the ceremony and informed me that at all costs, the parents had to be kept separated. We made it without further incident.

I seldom refuse to perform a ceremony because in spite of some of the unlikely candidates who appear for marriage, I am not their judge and at least they came to the Church. On one occasion however, as I went over the ceremony with the prospective couple, the young man demanded that all reference to prayer be omitted. When I asked why he said,

"I do not kneel before anybody." "Fine," I said, "Go find a justice of the peace, you are not getting married here."

In these days many marriages do not survive but it is gratifying to meet a couple years later who have been happy and successful and to know that you had an important part of a wonderful time in their lives

11

In Memoriam

"For everything there is a season, a time for every matter under heaven: a time to be born and a time to die..."
(ECCLESIASTES 3:1)

As we deal with the subject of death it is important to treat it with dignity and respect. At the same time we realize that in the experience and culture of dying we remain as human as we are in the happy and in-between times of our lives. From the standpoint of a pastor, the time of dying is a time to be present for those who need comfort, support and guidance. The words we say are never as important as the fact that we are there. Never hesitate to visit a home where grief has come for fear of not knowing what to say. Just go quickly and let them know that you care.

My first funeral came during the October before I finished college. I had never in my life attended a funeral. My Mother did not believe in taking children to funerals and so my Grandparents were buried without me. How was I going to handle this? For starters, I was aware that my soon bride to be, Phyllis, had attended many funerals as a teen ager because she often drove so that her parents could attend the services for neighbors and friends. Imagine having a date with your girl friend to discuss what they do at funerals. It happened to me.

The funeral happened this way. Mr. Brown was a prominent member of the community. He had been Church treasurer for 55 years. On the day that I went to meet with his family a hurricane passed through on an unusual route. I had never experienced a hurricane before so despite the radio weather reports and warnings, I set out anyway. As I turned the corner by the Church the motor drowned out. I got out of the car and was instantly soaked to the skin. Not to be deterred from my mission, I walked the next mile to the home. As I staggered in the door, the good Church ladies who were there gasped, sent me into a room and told me to take my clothes off and brought me pants and shirt belonging to the dead man who was considerably larger than I. They then hung my clothes behind the iron cook range in the kitchen where they remained for several days. I am not sure that I brought any consolation to the family but I surely provided them with a laugh.

On Saturday afternoon we went to the Church for the service. The parking lot was overflowing and there were license plates from several surrounding states as if I wasn't intimidated enough. I forged ahead and with the help of a couple very old, retired Baptist preachers it all went very well. The next day when we arrived at Church one of the members came over to the car, carrying my suit which was by now dry and as stiff as a board.

I have conducted many funeral services for people from all walks in life. Most are very similar, many are memorable for various reasons. There was the service for the man who suffered a heart attack while attempting to beat up his elderly father. There was the murder victim, shot in the street by his angry father-in law. There were the two victims of a spectacular car crash. There were times when the large Church Sanctuary could not hold all of the family and friends. Sadly, there were infants and the young teen aged victims of car crashes.

Sometimes a humorous comment during a funeral ceremony helps bring some comfort and insight. Sometimes it happens without your help. There was the family who came into the Church and on cue from the funeral director, all sat down at once only the pew kept sagging almost to the floor. There was the time when I went to the funeral home for the service of a man I had never met. I asked to see the family before the service began. As was my custom, I asked if there was anything they wanted me to know and particularly, were there any special passages of scripture they wanted me to read. The only response was, "Make it quick. He wasn't a religious man." They were out of there in seven minutes.

My brother who lives in a southern state once asked me, "Since you have been in both south and north, are funerals any different?" I told him, that they can be as nutty or as sane one place as another. Usually all is OK unless the service is planned by a family member who likes drama and lacks good taste. That was the case when the service for a rail road worker included a country band and a rousing rendition of, "Life Is Like A Mountain Railroad." Enough said.

None of the above includes the service in which I had no part other than to participate in a clergy procession. Time had been set aside at several points for persons present to come to the micro -phone and offer their thoughts and reminiscences. There were many, and some spoke for several minutes and often mostly about themselves. This went on for four hours!

In the end, what matters is the need to reach out and help in a time of grief and pain. Jesus did this with a few words and a loving heart. So must we.

12

Dinner Will Be Served

"And taking the five loaves and two fish he looked up to heaven, and blessed and broke them, and gave them to the disciples to set before the crowd. and all ate and were satisfied. And what was left over they gathered up, twelve baskets of broken pieces." (Luke 9:16–17)

It has been said that, "Where two or three Church people are gathered, there will be a dinner." Church dinners are part of our American culture but their origin goes back to scripture. The feeding of the 5,000 which was a miracle of loaves and fishes was a response to need. We understand that the early Christians worshipped in their homes, often around a meal. Our daily bread comes from God, surely God is present as it is served.

Where I grew up Church dinners served as fund raisers were many and the food was abundant. However, the fare at covered dish dinners while ample, usually consisted of the usual—baked beans, Jell-O, salad, bread and sheet cake. What an eye opener it was when my Southern Mother in-law invited us to a covered dish dinner at her Church. Handing me a box containing a carved ham she instructed me to put it in the car. Before I could get into the driver's seat, she called me back for another large box, fried chicken. Then she appeared with even more food. I wondered where the three of us were going to sit. Upon arriving at the Church it was evident that others had also brought great amounts of food. For these people, one could not do enough to create hospitality for family, friends and neighbors, especially when it was a matter of faith.

Church meals are most always enjoyable. My main complaint would be the weak coffee that is so typical of Church events. In one of my Churches I was actually forbidden to make the coffee. Come on folks—either make strong coffee or forget it! I also recall the time when my Father was visiting us and I took him with a group of men to a district men's dinner. The ladies of the host Church liked to brag about their special apple dumplings. That night I heard Dad looking around in the medicine cabinet. I asked what he needed. "Alka Seltzer, please" he said.

Then there was the time when we met for a covered dish dinner to launch the annual Week of Compassion offering for world hunger. As we were eating there was a loud crash. The food table had collapsed under the weight of our abundance. There is irony in there somewhere. Hopefully our special offering helped make abundance for others whose life was not so fortunate.

Over abundance is not always the case. As our Church hosted a district event one evening, there was a larger than expected attendance. Our Sunday School Superintendent who was serving as M C for the program happened to pass through the kitchen and overhear the concern of the ladies that the food could run short. Without a word to anyone else, he took it on himself to announce to the crowd that the attendance was larger than expected, "So please hit the refreshments light." The women were mortified.

Speaking of abundance and the lack thereof, I remember the time my Grandfather came home from a Church spaghetti dinner half mad and half laughing. These dinners were served by a family of truck driving brothers who used their special recipe given to them by an Italian customer in New York City. The diners were seated family style, ten to a table and the spaghetti was served on large platters overflowing with more than enough for all ten to help themselves. But on this night when the platter was set on the table, the first man to take it cleaned the whole platter onto his plate. Isn't there something in the Scriptures about the first shall be last and the last, first?

Our Men's Fellowship shared a monthly meeting which included a covered dish dinner. One member on a visit to his heart specialist who had placed him on a strict diet, bemoaned the fact that he might have to give up the monthly dinners he loved so much. The doctor said to him, "What you eat at Church won't hurt you." He proudly repeated that statement many times at our Church dinners. I like to think that there is truth in that statement. Scientifically, it sounds doubtful. However, I have quoted it often. "What you eat at Church won't hurt you."

13

Where Were You When.....

"For I am convinced that neither death, nor life, nor angels, nor rulers, nor things present nor things to come, nor powers, nor height, nor depth, nor anything else in all creation, will be able to separate us from the love of God in Christ Jesus our Lord." (Romans 8:38-39)

Life is a journey and none of us can accurately predict or always prepare for what happens next. This is true of our personal experience and it is true for cities, nations and all of civilization. The unexpected need to minister and represent a spiritual dimension to shattered lives or stunned crowds can arise at any moment. As a pastor one must always be ready to lend guidance, support, comfort, assurance and sensible interpretation to the events of personal tragedy or national disaster. To visit a grieving family or conduct a memorial service is something we can seldom write down ahead of time on our planning calendar. The resources for such events must usually be gathered quickly. Here is one reason that our personal faith and outlook must be nurtured and cared for constantly. Our response to grief, emergencies, the unexpected must be strong, helpful and grounded in faith.

Most of us in ministry can recall outstanding times when we were called on to minister, interpret, make sense of and offer faith and hope. It raises the question, Where were you when...?

On a November day in 1963, I was making a round of routine hospital visits. As I sat in the room of an elderly patient and passed the time in conversation, I overheard a nurse in the hallway say, "The president's been shot." That is all I heard and being preoccupied in my conversation, I paid little attention. But then as I left the hospital and got in my car, I thought of what I had heard and turned on the radio to find out. Sure enough, President Kennedy had been shot in Dallas. The very next day, the new President, Lyndon Johnson asked that everyone go to their own places of worship the following Monday and hold memorial services. I will never forget that service and the importance of it. Seldom have I seen Church members, choir members and deacons and elders volunteer so quickly to help out. In this time of national shock and mourning, this was one of the most important services I ever led.

This event led to something else I will never forget. A deacon in our Church, ex Marine and former Border Patrol officer was employed for a company near Washington D.C. When President Johnson declared a day of mourning and asked everyone to attend a place of worship, this man's boss threatened to fire anyone who missed work and attended worship. My friend came to Church anyway and yes, he was fired. Later he was reinstated when corporate headquarters learned of it but his integrity and willingness to take a stand are unforgettable.

There were other occasions I recall speaking out or reaching out. The assassination of Dr. Martin Luther King Jr., the end of the Vietnam war, the Sunday after a shocking murder in our community to mention a few. Of course, ranking up there next to the assassination of JFK was what we now call 9/11. On a spectacularly beautiful Tuesday Morning we watched the TV with horror at what was happening at the twin towers, the Pentagon and the skies over Pennsylvania. We quickly organized a prayer service at the Church for that evening and just like it had been in another time and place in 1963, Church members scrambled to be of help. That time of prayer and reflection did not ease our sadness over what had just happened but it strengthened our faith and reminded us that in spite of evil, God is with us. {*"Even though we walk through the valley of the shadow of death, we will fear no evil for God is with us..."*}

14

Faith Makes The Difference

"For my thoughts are not your thoughts, nor are your ways my ways, says the Lord. For as the heavens are higher than the earth, so are my ways higher than your ways and my thoughts than your thoughts." (ISAIAH 55:8–9)

"The steadfast love of the Lord never ceases, his mercies never come to an end; They are new every morning; great is your faithfulness." (LAMENTATIONS 3:22–23)

Why do we concern ourselves with these issues of Faith, Church and Ministry? What makes it so important? The answer is—Faith Makes The Difference. It is a proven fact that individuals who embrace something or someone out there beyond themselves and acknowledge a spiritual presence are more fulfilled in their living and their sense of purpose in life and day to day living. We are more than the flesh and blood of our bodies or the nerve system we call the brain. We are the creation of a greater one who besides designing our physical attributes and giving us life, breathed into us a spirit and the ability to reach out and embrace truth, love and an awareness of God. Our human understandings of who or what God is, may differ but we are all the creation of a power and wisdom and genius far greater than ourselves. Besides the opportunities for prayer, meditation, reflection and observation there is the gathered community of believers. In this community of faith we can share our common observations and beliefs, find inspiration and hope and give meaning to our faith as we live out the mandates of compassion, justice and love. Without faith, life can be shallow, empty and a constant search for hope and meaning that goes on unsatisfied and incomplete. Faith makes the difference between emptiness and fulfillment, despair and hope, darkness and light, idleness and purpose, inner turmoil and inner peace. I have found these truths to be well worthy of my efforts to study, teach, preach and minister in the name of the Christ who calls people to meaningful discipleship.

You do not need to have lived very long to know that the growth and pace of technology happens incredibly fast. Sometimes this week's new discovery makes last week's latest product obsolete. The way we communicate today was not imagined just a few years ago. Yesterday's science fiction is today's reality. Day by day, medical discoveries unleash treatments or cures for diseases that not long ago were a death sentence. We continue to learn how to nourish ourselves and take care of ourselves so that life is healthier and longer.

Every day, the mysteries of the universe are revealed with discoveries of more galaxies, unknown planets and the continuing explosion of ongoing creation. Knowledge literally explodes around us. Does this mean that as human beings we are becoming more intelligent, more powerful, more creative and less dependent on the idea of a divine being or spiritual need? Quite the contrary. The more we discover and the more we are able to know and understand, the deeper and greater the mysteries of God become. We did not create these things by ourselves, there is the creator who makes it all possible for us to discover and know. The deeper we probe into space the greater the evidence of God becomes.

Knowledge and discovery entail great human study and effort and yet they are also gifts. We are blessed by what we can know about the universe or the ways we can communicate or heal disease but there is a source for all of this and it is incumbent upon us to seek that source and be in touch with it. All of these wonders originate from a power and intelligence beyond human comprehension—we call it God. The greater our knowledge and accomplishments, the greater the evidence of God becomes.

One of the greatest resources for faith and spiritual knowledge and awareness is the Bible. None of our modern discoveries, technology, or understandings render the Bible out of date nor do they relegate it to the area of obsolete thinking or superstition. On the contrary, if we understand the Bible in an enlightened manner, we find here a source of wisdom, power and insight that makes our modern day discoveries and knowledge even more powerful. Some of what appears there may seem quaint along side of modern life today. Some of it can be seen as mythological. That does not remove God from the picture and it does not take away the basic truth being represented. Whether the details of some events or Bible stories stand the test of scientific knowledge is not relevant. Truth is revealed in faith stories as well as in events that stand the scrutiny of historical accuracy. The Genesis story of creation is a sheer work of genius. The very order of what was created follows good science and even evolution. Note that it begins with water, progresses through vegetation and various form of life until the highest life form of all appears—human beings. Adam and Eve did not discover God, God revealed himself to them. Their fall from grace through disobedience is the story of human society down through the ages to the present time. We need to listen to God. There are consequences when we do not. Whether you understand the couple in the Garden of Eden to be actual historical figures or heroes of a faith legend makes no difference. They still represent the truth and the fact that we are God's creation with a divine origin and a divine purpose. Read on through the stories of Noah, Abraham and others and what is important here is that God was continuing to reveal himself to all humanity through the most believable means possible—human beings themselves.

As the story of where we came from and who we are progresses we reach a point where tribes are established, communities are formed and neighborhoods bring people into close association with each other. If this is to happen without chaos and strife boundaries must be established and laws must guide and protect them. Out of the mayhem of bondage and disorganization, the tribes of Israel find themselves in need of law and order. In one of the Bible's most dramatic moments Moses is summoned to the top of Mt. Sinai where he receives from the hand of God the tablets of the law. We know them today as the Ten Commandments. In one sense this set of laws is not unique in that similar codes emerged from other cultures and nations. What sets the laws given to Moses apart is that they begin with our relationship with God and from this connection our relationship with one another is defined. The first four commandments set the conditions of our relationship with God. Holiness, awe, respect and honor. This being said, we go to the remaining six laws dealing with how we live with our family, neighbors and the wider community. In these rules for living, essential for meaningful life in any community or society are embodied the sacredness of our creator and the divine – human encounter. There is more. Our behavior with and toward one another is founded on a respect for the divine in everyone. That spirit originates with God the creator. In short, we must respect each other because we respect God our creator. When Jesus was challenged by his adversaries concerning his knowledge and respect for the law, he summed it all up with a further mandate from Moses,

> *"You shall love the Lord your God with all your heart, and with all your soul and with all your mind". This is the greatest and first commandment. And a second is like it." You shall love your neighbor as yourself." On these two commandments hang all the law and the prophets."*
> (Matthew 22:37–40)

Jesus makes it clear that the basis of our relationship with one another in this world begins with our love and respect for God.

There are numerous accounts of battles, wars, kings and armies. One can easily get lost in the details about who fought the Philistines and when. However the underlying truth in all of this is that faith was being defended because faith matters. Note that in all of this the exploits of kings and soldiers alike come under the scrutiny of a concerned and just God.

The Biblical story of ancient Israel represents the triumph and tragedy of any nation. What makes this story so important is the emergence of prophets who in the name of a righteous, yet loving God confronted corruption, idolatry, greed and evil with severe warnings. They challenged their hearers to pay attention to God and that same summons stands for us today. The prophets decried the false values and the moral decay that destroys society and challenged their original hearers as they challenge us to *"Seek the Lord, while he may be found..."* Amidst the shambles of all that can go wrong in a life or a nation the prophetic voices ring loud and clear with a call to integrity, accountability, peace, justice and a meaningful faith. To us these prophets may seem strange and eccentric at times. They were people with strange sounding names speaking to the realities of life as it was then. They remain a powerful voice to be listened to and heard and applied to the conditions of our own time as well.

Tucked in the middle of the Old Testament are the writings of sensitive spirits who expressed their deep awareness of God in Psalms and Hymns that speak to the soul of people in any generation. These are people who see not only a sunrise but the hand of God, who observe not only a shepherd and sheep but God and his people. They speak from their highs and lows and still understand that whatever the day may bring, God is here. When they arise in the morning they greet God and when they lie down to rest it is with a prayer of gratitude. God is their source of forgiveness, comfort and hope. Indeed God is the source of their sanity. They dared claim for themselves the compassionate mercies of God. What a gift to know that they have passed these insights and understandings on to us. How wonderful to know that their words are as relevant today as when they were first voiced or written. We are God's people. Spiritual beings and nowhere are we reminded of this more than in the writings of these people of insight and faith.

The pinnacle of all of this is Jesus Christ. There is no higher or nobler expression of who we were created to be and what we are expected to do than is represented in his teaching and life. The beautiful stories of Jesus' birth are an impressive way of saying that here was one sent from God with a purpose. Here was evidence that we are not abandoned but loved by God. But what gives these stories real importance is the life Jesus lived, the teaching he shared and his willingness to stand to the death in order to wrest faith and salvation from the grasp of a few elite would be guardians of truth and offer them freely to all who would sincerely come. In this, Jesus is truly the Son of God. He is the genuine expression of God who reaches out to all of us and whose will is to exclude no one. Jesus becomes our Savior by showing us the love of God and teaching us what God would have us do and how to live with one another. As important as eternity may be to our faith and our hope, Jesus helps us understand that we must first live in the here and now and he shows us how.

One thing that lends credibility to all of this is the fact that whatever title he may have borne Jesus was truly human. As he sought to prepare himself for the stupendous ministry ahead, he went alone into the wilderness to meditate and pray. It was there that he was tempted to turn his back on the whole thing and forget it. We too would feel the same fears and anxieties. Yet he overcame those thoughts, not with ease or uncaring but with the same agonizing thoughtfulness that would be required of any of us. His clashes with those who opposed him were no easier than such encounters would be for us. His pain and suffering through betrayal, trial, flogging and crucifixion were every bit as hard for him as it would be for any of us. In no way was he ever exempt from the conditions we all live in.

I was born in the twentieth century and now live in the twenty first. I benefit from all of the modern technology, discoveries and knowledge that are exploding around us. The marvels of science and technology show amazing human achievement but they also reveal a creative source beyond ourselves. With all that we are able to learn, create and accomplish, there are things beyond our comprehension and which defy any scientific analysis. I believe in the resurrection of Jesus Christ. I believe that he was crucified and buried and then appeared to those who loved him and were able to see him with eyes of faith. Evil will be defeated. God's love will prevail. Death can not claim us in the end. God will. I have even read accounts of people who attempted to explain Jesus' resurrection in some scientific way. Forget it! It defies our human knowledge. But know this—Jesus lives and that is real. No amount of evil can destroy the hope of Easter Sunday. No amount of laboratory analysis or think tank discussion can unwrap the mystery of Jesus' resurrection. Christ is alive! Thank God!

What They Can't Teach You In Preacher School

"For this reason I remind you to rekindle the gift of God that is within you through the laying on of my hands; for God did not give us a spirit of cowardice but a spirit of power and love and of self discipline." (II TIMOTHY 1:6–7)

There is much that is not taught in a minister's formal education no matter how many years it lasts or how many degrees earned. As I stated earlier, there is no substitute for the years spent in study and formal learning and any pastor who does not read on a regular basis is lowering his/her effectiveness and skills. What is not taught in seminary classes is due to no lack of vision or prejudice or omission. It is not taught because it can't be taught. Life happens—therefore a pastor's life consists of constant on the job training. There are many events, incidents and surprise happenings which we must deal with without training wheels. Life, after all is a living thing and living things are not predictable.

No matter where you are on your journey in life or your professional experience, the most memorable learnings will come unexpectedly. Read the Bible, read what reputable sources say, but most of all, look, listen and pray. Scripture reminds us that when we have no resources of our own, the Spirit intercedes for us, even prays for us. How else could we answer "yes" to our impossible calling? It works.

After a lifetime of ministry, I remain convinced—The Church is here to stay and the call is still out there

"Whom shall I send and who will go for us?... Here am I, send me." (ISAIAH 6:8)

SERMON : *The Proving Ground*

I Corinthians 3:1–15

Life is full of stories and events—some worth telling about – some not. Some are significant and meaningful—others, shallow and meaningless. Keeping up with world events and life changing issues is important. On the other hand the so-called news about some celebrity's wardrobe or their latest immoral antics is not news, it is trash. We need to discern which stories we hear, see or read are important and what isn't. Life can be filled with meaning. Without God life can be meaningless and empty.

But even as life is filled with the stories that we see, hear, read and tell, there is still another story being told—your story and my story. No matter what else goes on in the world, you have a story too. You may not view it as remarkable or exciting or outstanding but it is your story and it is being written each day. Your story is being tested—not for facts, excitement and not in any way comparing it to someone else's story. It is being tested for meaning and for value. One day as I spoke with the family of a man who had passed away regarding his funeral service, they told me to make it quick. For some reason this man's life meant so little to them that they could not spend a few moments to honor his memory. What they were saying was, "His life wasn't important, let's get it over with and get out of here." But that was their judgment, it was not that poor man's judgment and certainly not God's judgment. Surely somewhere in this person's life was something of value or some brief moment of goodness. We don't always know from outward or casual appearances. We do know that every day life is being proven and tested as it is lived.

In the first letter to the Church at Corinth, Paul who had worked with the congregation for some time, speaks of the quality of the spiritual and congregational life. He cautions them against divisions and petty differences. He reminds them that the real issue is Christ and how they represent Christ as a Church and as individuals. He speaks of his own life and work among them saying,

> *"According to the grace of God given to me, like a skilled master builder, I laid a foundation and someone else is building upon it. Each builder must choose with care how to build on it.*
>
> *For no one can lay any foundation other than the one that has been laid; that foundation is Jesus Christ'*

(I CORINTHIANS 3:10–11)

The materials we put into life, the foundation of that life, the quality of our lives will determine whether or not our life and our work will stand the test. On this Labor Day weekend which is set aside to honor working people and the work they do, it is appropriate to think about what it is we do with whatever God has given us. I speak not only of how we make a living but how we live our lives. This includes the total picture of life, work and faith. What does your life mean? What does it stand for and can it pass the test? What kind of story are you telling from day to day? In his letter, Paul continues speaking of how we build on the foundation of Christ.

> *"Now if anyone builds on the foundation with gold, silver, precious stones, wood, hay, straw —*
>
> *the work of each builder will become visible, for the day will disclose it because it will be*
>
> *revealed with fire and the fire will test what sort of work each one has done. If the work which*
>
> *any one has built on the foundation survives, the builder will receive a reward. If the work is burned up the builder will suffer loss; the builder will be saved but through fire."* (I CORINTHIANS 3:12–15)

What does this mean? I think Paul is saying that we are not to be the judge of another's life and work. Rather, we are all subject to the judgment of God and that is revealed in the test of time and life and results. In fact there is no way to fully know how much good we may do as we live lives of faithfulness and love.

The test is in the living. The proving ground is life itself and the final decisions are in the hands of God. Some large companies put their workers through an annual evaluation to determine the value of their work and possibly the future of their employment. Comments are received from co-workers and supervisors as well as records of actual productivity. After review, the employee is called in to go over these results. It must be a trying experience to go through. But whether that happens to us or not, in the big picture, our life is revealed before God every day. So what are you telling? What does your life reveal? Is it worthwhile or is it empty? Is at least some part of your story worth repeating?

One summer I bought an extra fan for our home. We plugged it in and let it start running. It started off ok but later when we came back into the room there was the smell of burnt electrical coil. The fan had stopped running and was very hot to the touch. I took it back to the store to return it. No questions asked. The clerk had my refund money ready almost before I reached the counter. Then I noticed a whole pile of the same kind of fans stacked there. In spite of the leading brand name or the claims printed on the box, all were defective. They looked great in the store but they did not pass the test of use and time. I was reminded of Paul's example of being tested by fire.

The story that we tell and the story we live will be worthwhile and meaningful when they are built on the foundation that Paul speaks of—Jesus Christ. His is the greatest story in the world and it affects all of us. So the lines of a beloved hymn include these words,

> I love to tell the story,
> More wonderful it seems
> Than all the golden fancies
> Of all our golden dreams.
> (Katherine Hankey)

This is the most wonderful story in the world and we can know more about it, we can come to understand it, and we can share in it as our own. First, we can read Matthew, Mark, Luke and John. We can take it as the light and example of our own life and hope. And we can live it. When the truth of Christ becomes the truth by which we live, we begin to live the story. When the justice and peace, love and non-violence that Christ lived and died for become our goal also, we are living the story. When love and forgiveness replace hate and bitterness within us we are living the story. When the foundation of Christ becomes the foundation of our family and of how we do business or what we do with our life at work or away from work, we are living the story. When others can see something of Christ in us without ever having to mention it, we are living the story. When our Church, our neighborhood, our work place, or wherever it is we are involved in are better because we are there, we are living the story. This story is indeed worth more than,

"All the golden fancies of all our golden dreams."

The quality of life is in part documented by what that life stands for and for what it means to others. I remember another funeral service I was called on to conduct. That service included two pastors, a guest quartet of singers and all sorts of moaning and groaning among the family. The fact was that this man died of a heart attack in a drunken rage attempting to beat up his 76 year old father. No amount of preaching, praying or singing is going to change that. The story was already written. We can only hope that somewhere in that man's forty nine years there was some good. The point is, we need to take more seriously our part in the old story of Jesus Christ. We need to make his story more a part of our story.

Like you, I have met people who disappoint or turn out to be other than they appeared. But they are outnumbered by so many whose story will never make headlines but who showed faith and courage, love, growth and compassion. There was the lady in her early fifties who knew death for her was a short time off. She said to me, "I don't fear what is coming. It will be like moving into the next room." I remember also, the family who went out in their car in a Sunday morning snowstorm and somehow picked up twenty two people and brought them to Church. I have seen eighty year old women take part in a walkathon to raise money to fight muscular dystrophy, I have listened to a one hundred and one year Sunday School teacher recite the name of every child she taught in Sunday School from 1910 – 1970. I have had conversations with Church members who may not have been formally educated but spoke with eloquent words of wisdom because they knew the story and were living it. I have witnessed incredible selfishness but I have also seen incredible love and sacrifice. I have seen people give of their time, energy and resources because they believed in the story and knew that God had important things for them to do. The letter to the Hebrews provides a long list of love and sacrifices made by faithful people and then says to us,

> *"Therefore, since we are surrounded by so great a cloud of witnesses, let us also lay aside every weight and sin which clings so closely, and let us run with perseverance, the race that is set before us, looking to Jesus, the pioneer and perfecter of our faith, who for the sake of the joy that was set before him, endured the cross, disregarding its shame, and is seated at the right hand of the throne of God."* (HEBREWS 12:1–2)

Looking to Jesus whose story we can learn and live. The story that brings meaning to every day that we live. His story is our story. We can live it now.

SERMON : *I Love To Tell The Story*
Isaiah 6:1 – 8, Luke 5:1 – 11, Romans 10:5- 17

*"But how are men to call upon him in whom they have
not believed? And how are they to believe in one of whom
they have never heard? And how are they to hear without
someone to proclaim him? And how are they to proclaim
him unless they are sent?....So faith comes from what is
heard and what is heard comes through the word of Chrst."*
(ROMANS 10:14–15, 17)

"I love to tell the story of unseen things above,
of Jesus and his glory, of Jesus and his love, I
love to tell the story, because I know it's true;
it satisfies my longings as nothing else can do."

(Katherine Hankey)

These words of Paul to the Romans along with the words
of a favorite old hymn describe my story since leaving high
school and perhaps somewhat before. Growing up as the
oldest child of a pastor, I probably had insights and saw
things that few kids know about. My mother used to tell
about me when I was around 5. I would gather together
some imaginary people and conduct a wedding. Then there
was the Sunday when I was about ten when all four of us
kids had colds and were not sent to Sunday School. So, I
went down in the basement and found a couple boxes and
made my own pulpit and got my new Bible out and with the
whole captive audience my Mother, Brother and two Sisters,
sitting on the couch, we had Church. Then there was the
time when my sixth grade teacher was encouraging us to be
confident in public speaking. I was a very shy kid. —really.
She handed me a very funny poem to read and as I read it
loudly and clearly the class burst into laughter and the more
I read the louder they laughed and I am thinking, Yes! I can

do this! Later, when I was preparing for college I became aware of the words we read from Isaiah this morning,

> *"Whom shall I send and who will go for us? And I said, "Here am I; send me!"* (ISAIAH 6:8)

Then there are Jesus' words spoken to the fishermen down by the lake,

> *"Do not be afraid; from now on you will be catching people."* (LUKE 5:10)

Five Churches later and with more experiences than I have time to tell, here I am. So that's my story—so far. But if you think my story is a one man act, think again. From the very beginning Phyllis has been half of my story living from day to day with incredible generosity and wisdom. I tell you the truth when I say that the first funeral I ever attended, I conducted. Phyllis had to tell me what they do at funerals. Did you ever meet your girlfriend for a date and spend the evening learning what they do at funerals? You have to say, it's different. Talk about on the job training! Believe me that was just the first of way more than a thousand I conducted. I am thinking that the title of the book I plan to write should be, "Look—No Training Wheels!" Later on it was Phyllis who convinced me that I could leave my written sermon home and speak without notes. It worked. For many years in our last Church Phyllis was employed as Church Secretary but it was much more. Soon it included financial records and it was not long before people, especially women found a friend with whom they could counsel and confide. When I was out of town and a death or other emergency happened, she would go and make that visit in my place. And it was not just me who held some important denominational offices. She served on The Regional Board and on several committees in Virginia and then two terms on the National General Board of the Disciples of Christ. This has been and continues to be her ministry and her story too. All this while raising a son we could be proud of.

You have a story also. Yours is different than ours. We are all different but we all have a story and whether or not we think it is important or worth mentioning, it is our story and maybe when you think about it, it is more remarkable than you realize. Maybe you should tell your story too.

But there is a story that is bigger than all of us – it is God's story. As a book by one of my old seminary professors proclaims, "God Has A Story Too." That is what this book we call the Bible is all about but God's story is far too big to be contained in any book even this one. God's story is everywhere and in every age including ours. God's story never ends. We UCC people like to repeat the phrase, "God is still speaking." And we are right in doing so for God never stops speaking. In every sunrise and sunset, in every lesson learned by humanity, in every effort to seek justice and peace, in your faith and mine, God is still speaking. God's story never ends. A couple years ago I was amused when I attended a meeting which was opened with devotions by a Conference Minister. Now all due respect to the man, I am sure he didn't think about what he was saying but he opened by saying that he was reading from his new Bible. It was a so called "green" Bible printed on recycled, biodegradable paper. Well who needs a biodegradable Bible! What's the purpose of it? The first thing that popped into my mind was the words of the prophet,

> "The grass withers, the flower fades but the word of our God stands forever."

So great and vast and beyond all human comprehension is God's story. That story has to be told.

Someone has to tell it. That story was written for us, it was given to us and it includes us. That story goes on. It is more than just the old, old story, it is the living chronicle of the living God.

That is why Paul says,

> "But how are they to call on one in whom they have not believed? And how are they to believe in one of whom they have never heard? And how are they to hear without someone to proclaim him? And how are they to proclaim him unless they are sent?....So faith comes from what is

heard and what is heard comes from the word of Christ."
(ROMANS 10:14–15, 17)

This is what I have been about and this is what I continue to be about. But in some way, God calls on all of us to share his story, if not in the Church or from the pulpit, with our daily lives and in the way we take the teaching of Christ seriously enough to live it our in practical experience which is what it was intended for. I love to tell the story—why? As the song goes,

"...what seems each time I tell it, more wonderfully sweet."

Then another verse,

"...for those who know it best seem hungering and thirsting to hear it like the rest."

Not all the need in our lives is physical. There is that deep inner need that only God can reach. What about the five thousand people who gathered on a Galilean hillside to listen to Jesus speak all day? Didn't they have something else to do? You bet they did but nothing could take the place of the eternal word, wisdom, encouragement, light and hope that comes from God's story. Don't you have other things you could be doing on most Sunday mornings? Of course, but nothing else can take the place of worship in God's house and the renewal of your spirit, so you come to this place as others go to their place of worship because of your own need and because the Spirit of God calls. "And how are they to hear without a preacher?"

God has a story too and it is our business to know it, to tell it and to live it but nobody can tell that story alone.

Let me remind you that we are the Church, the community of believers called by Paul, the body of Christ. That says to us, we are all in this together. What would the Church be if we were all preachers or Church officers or Lord forbid, seminary professors? We are the Church—all of us. Telling the story is more than the responsibility of a few. Take time to learn the story. Come to Church. Here is a novel idea—READ

THE BIBLE. You might not understand all of it but at least learn about Jesus and what he has to say about our daily living and our relationship with God and how God wants us to live with each other and in the world. Knowing the story and telling the story is the business of all of us. How we tell the story depends on the experiences and opportunities that come into our own lives. We tell it in the way we live and care, in our patience, understanding and love and our willingness now and then to speak a good word for Jesus Christ. How many people do we invite to Church? How often do we speak an encouraging word of faith to someone? We don't have to be like those obnoxious people who go around knocking on doors or stopping people on the street and ask, "Are you saved?" To me that is not telling the story it is in your face meddling. I certainly do not appreciate the people who demonstrate and obstruct traffic or carry their placards around for some cause or opinion. They appear to be a bunch of spoiled babies whining and complaining that nobody made their world perfect. Of course it isn't perfect so we are called to tell and live the story of Jesus and his love in the everyday places of life where it will be meaningful and effective. The world will be closer to perfect when we get out there and tell and live the story. Jesus gave his life on the cross. That was not just a statement or a demonstration or just to find out if you have been saved. He gave his life because he stood against the forces of evil and destruction for our sake. He died on the cross to bring God into your life. In his own words,

> *"Greater love has no one than this, that a man lay down his life for his friends."*

That is why the story is so important and why it must be told. That is why we have preachers, pastors and Church members. In Christ, not only have we discovered something too important to ignore in our lives, it is too important not to love it, to live and to tell it to anyone who comes our way. We tell it in our words or in our actions but we are all called to tell the story. It is God's story and it is our story and the story goes on forever!

This Book is Dedicated with Love and Gratitude
To
My Wife, Phyllis
without whose Love, Support,
Encouragement and Partnership this Ministry
would not be possible

www.ingramcontent.com/pod-product-compliance
Lightning Source LLC
Chambersburg PA
CBHW062026040426
42447CB00010B/2157